FAMILY TIME
TRAINING

Bible
Activities
and Object
Lessons
for Families
with
Preschoolers

Bubbles, Balloons, & Chocolate

KIRK WEAVER

To Jim Weidmann, who introduced me to the priceless joy and peace that comes from providing intentional spiritual training in the home. To my family—Kelly, Madison, and McKinley—who have embraced Family Time as a core value in our life together. And, to our unborn grandchildren and great-grandchildren, may you learn, live, and teach Jesus as our personal Savior and eternal hope.

To Ed and Lisa Janich, who have allowed God to direct their lives in such a way that thousands have been blessed. Their attentiveness to the leading of God's Spirit has opened doors of opportunity. To God be the glory for connecting Ed and Lisa with Family Time Training.

—*Kirk Weaver*

Table of Contents

Family Activities

   Teaching Goal: God gave Jesus power over death.
   Scripture: John 11:1-44

   Teaching Goal: Friends provide support.
   Scripture: Exodus 17:8-13

   Teaching Goal: God wants us to share the Good News about Jesus
      with others.
   Scripture: Matthew 4:18-22, Acts 3:11-26, Matthew 28:16-20

   Teaching Goal: Even though we cannot see God, he is there
      and he is powerful!
   Scripture: John 6:46, Romans 1:20

   Teaching Goal: The Word of God is sweet, helping us overcome
      stubbornness and rebelliousness.
   Scripture: Ezekiel 2 and 3, Ezekiel 3:1-3

   Teaching Goal: Jesus suffered for our sin, died, and rose again,
      conquering death so that we might join him in heaven.
   Scripture: Matthew 27-28, Luke 24

   Teaching Goal: The story of Dorcas teaches us the value of serving others.
   Scripture: 1 Corinthians 13:4, Acts 9:36-42

   Teaching Goal: The story of David teaches us that God can
      protect us against big challenges.
   Scripture: 1 Samuel 17

Mission

The mission of Family Time Training is to reach future generations with the Good News of Christ by training parents to teach their children Christian principles, values, and beliefs in the home.

Vision Statement

Imagine a child who responds to the needs of others and is eager to give and share.

Imagine a child who has learned to say "no" to busyness. A child who will take time to slow down and who understands the necessity of Sabbath rest.

Imagine a child who has been trained to seek truth.

Imagine a child who lives accountable to an unseen but always present God.

Imagine a child whose best friend is Jesus.

Imagine a child who is more eager to learn about the teachings of Jesus than to watch television or play sports.

Imagine a child with an eternal perspective, a child who invests more time giving and serving than accumulating and being entertained.

Imagine hundreds and thousands, a whole generation, of children growing up to live and teach the example of Christ.

In Deuteronomy 6:7 God presents his plan for passing on a godly heritage to our children. At Family Time Training our vision is to see future generations living for Christ. First, parents are to be the primary spiritual teachers in the lives of children. Second, spiritual training is to take place 24 hours a day, seven days a week. Family Time Training is just a tool, but it is a tool God can use in your family to accomplish his vision.

Foreword

"I believe most parents who are Christian want to teach their children the faith, they just don't know how. The church is important support but primary spiritual teaching must happen in the home, otherwise, it's not going to happen."

—R.C. Sproul, theologian

Family Time is the "how to" tool parents can use to teach their children the faith at home. The organization Family Time Training equips parents with fun and exciting activities designed to teach children Christian principles, values, and beliefs.

Family Time Training was formed in response to a spiritual crisis that threatens to undermine the foundation of today's families. For generations, Christian parents have abdicated to the church their God-given role as the primary spiritual leaders for their children. The church is expected to build within the lives of children a strong spiritual foundation in just one or two hours per week. God designed spiritual training to take place 24 hours a day, seven days a week, with the parents providing primary leadership and the church providing important support. For the sake of our children we must return proactive spiritual training to the home.

Family Time Training works with churches, schools, and spiritually-based groups to teach parents how to provide home-based spiritual training. Training is provided through sermons, classes, and weekend seminars. Families receive direct support through a website (www.famtime.com), activity books, and quarterly mailings.

—Kirk Weaver

Introduction

Not long ago, my wife Kelly and I were talking with Madison on her bed in her room. She was upset with the kids at school. Some were picking on an unpopular student, playing a cruel game Madi chose not to play, and it left her separated from her girlfriends. With tears flowing down her face, Madi said, "I'm trying to be like the beans in Dad's story."

Madi was referring to a Family Time lesson. The activity is built around three pots of boiling water, with the water representing adversity. We drop a carrot into the first pot, an egg into the second, and coffee beans into the third. What choices will we make in response to the adversity we face in our lives? Do we get soft like the carrot the way Peter did when he denied Christ? Does the adversity make us hard like the egg and Pharaoh's heart? Or like the coffee beans, which can represent the example of Paul, do we influence and change the environment around us? Madi was applying a lesson that we'd taught more than four months earlier.

As a parent, you've had moments like this. You know what they're worth.

Family Time activities are simple, fun object lessons intended to teach children about life in God's world. This is a book of ideas for structured teaching times that will carry forward and open doors for informal learning moments. At first it may feel a little clumsy to create the structured time, to boil carrots and eggs and coffee beans. But the moments when your child actively chooses the godly path will fuel your love and your relationship like nothing else in the world.

"Here's the game," I told the four children, my son, daughter, and two neighborhood friends. They were standing at the bottom of the stairs, wide-eyed and eager for the Family Time activity. Standing at the top of the stairs, I said, "I represent Jesus in heaven. More than anything I want you up here with me, but, you can't use the stairs and you can't use the handrails."

They knew there was a trick, something to learn. But what? How would they get from the bottom of the stairs to the top without touching the stairs or the railing? My daughter ran to get a laundry basket, turned it upside down, stood on top and reached up only to find she was still more than fifteen steps from the top.

It was my son, Mac, the youngest of the four, who figured out the solution. "I got it! Dad, please come down and get me," his face beaming, because he had solved the riddle. I descended the stairs.

"Will you carry me to the top?" he asked. "Of course!" I responded. After carrying all four children piggyback style to the second floor, I said, "That's how you get to heaven. You can't do it on your own. Only through Jesus can you get there." A powerful lesson presented in the language of children that they still remember to this day.

Deuteronomy 6:5-9 says:
> *"Love the LORD your God with all your heart and with all your soul and with all your strength. These commandments that I give you today are to be upon your hearts. Impress them on your children."*

How?
> *"Talk about them when you sit at home and when you walk along the road, when you lie down and when you get up. Tie them as symbols on your hands and bind them on your foreheads. Write them on the doorframes of your houses and on your gates."*

How will we shape our children? What mark will we leave upon them? Is it possible that we can launch them into the world stronger, purer, more trusting of God than we were? Is it possible that we can reshape our families and our family interactions around the joy of loving God with all that is within us?

I believe it is possible. That's what this book is for.

The ABC's of Effective Family Times

A **Attention Span:** The rule of thumb for attention span is one minute for each year of age. A three-year-old may have a three-minute attention span. Break up your Family Time into three-minute increments. With variety, you gain additional attention span. For example:

3 minutes	Sing or play your Family Time theme song
2 minutes	Pray
3 minutes	Tell the story
3 minutes	Demonstrate the object lesson
3 minutes	Let the child repeat the object lesson
3 minutes	Retell the story
2 minutes	Practice memorization
2 minutes	Close in prayer

21 minutes	Total Family Time

B **Be Prepared to Say "I Don't Know":** Your children WILL ask you a question that you cannot answer. Promise to find the answer and get back to them within 24 hours. You can call a pastor or search the Internet for more information.

C **Call it Family Time:** When your children grow up you want them to have fond, lasting memories of Family Time. When referring to your times of formal spiritual training, say "Family Time" often. In the same way your children will remember going to school and church or playing sports and music, they will remember times of spiritual training called "Family Time."

D **Drama Queens and Kings:** Kids love to put on plays. Pick a Bible Story, assign the roles from Director to Diva—everyone gets in on the act. Don't forget to assign a videographer so you can watch it later.

When is our family time?

E Encourage Guessing: Answering a question involves risk. Your child's answer may be right or wrong. Praise him when he guesses at an answer. If he gives the wrong answer say, "Great guess! The answer is..." and give him the correct information. This will keep him participating. If you say, "No, that's wrong," children may eventually stop talking.

F Fixed or Flexible: It's great and admirable to have Family Time the same night every week. However, it may not be practical for your family. Be willing to move the night if needed. The important thing is to have at least one Family Time each week.

G Give it to God: God commands parents and grandparents to be spiritual teachers with their children (Deuteronomy 6:7; Deuteronomy 4:9, Psalm 78:5). Trust that God will equip you to fulfill his plan. As you prepare, and before you begin your Family Time each week, pray and ask the Holy Spirit to lead you and clearly communicate the message to your children.

H Hold the Distractions: When sitting at the table, remove the centerpiece, pencils, paper...anything that can distract a child. A random paper clip left on a table can lead to a possession battle that will ruin the atmosphere for Family Time. Also, when using materials like balloons, string, etc., don't bring them out until you're ready to use them.

I Involve Kids in the Preparations: Whenever possible, especially as kids get a little older, involve kids in the lesson preparations. Preparation can be as much fun as doing the activity and certainly increases ownership. Kids will enjoy making an obstacle course, building a tent with sheets, or mixing a big batch of cornstarch.

J Just Do It!: Don't wait another day to get started!

K Kitchen Table: Start your Family Time at the kitchen table even if you are only going to be there for a few minutes. Chairs provide natural boundaries that will help children focus as you explain what will happen during the Family Time.

Listen to the Holy Spirit: Be prepared to modify or change the discussion if the Spirit moves the conversation in a different direction.

Make a Picture: Coloring a picture to reinforce a Bible Story can be an excellent teaching technique. While the family is coloring, great conversation about the lesson can take place.

Not a Spectator Sport: Participate with your children in the game or activity. By participating, you show your kids that you value Family Time.

Oh Boy! If you're feeling frustrated or if family members have a negative attitude—reschedule. Keep it positive.

Play it Again, Sam: For younger children, put the lesson into a one sentence phrase like: "Noah had faith in God." Or, "Be content with what God sent." The same night at bedtime, remind children of the main point. The following morning ask them what they remember from Family Time the night before.

Quitting isn't an Option: Commit to once a week and do your best not to take a week off. Continue to do Family Time during the summer months. If you stop, your kids will sense a lack of commitment to Family Time on your part.

Repetition isn't the Same as Redundant: Younger children learn best through repetition. In the same way they will watch a video over and over, they may want to repeat fun Family Time activities. Be prepared to repeat the activity, asking the children to explain what the different elements represent. Consider repeating with neighborhood children; your children will learn even more when they teach others.

Simple Structure: Younger children benefit from a structured time together. Consider following the Family Time Format each week.

T **To Be or Not to Be Silly:** Model for your children that it's okay to be dramatic, silly, and have fun. Kids love it when their parents are playful.

U **Unique Locations:** Have a church service in a crawl space to represent the early church under persecution. Hold your Family Time outside at a neighborhood park. Repeat fun activities when visiting relatives on vacation. Tell the story of Zacchaeus while sitting in a tree house. Changing the setting of your Family Time can be fun.

V **Variety:** Using a video clip can be an excellent way to teach a lesson. However, using video clips three weeks in a row becomes predictable and is less effective. Mix up the format and tools you use in your weekly Family Time (coloring, video clips, a snack tied to the lesson, etc.).

W **Watch Out for Unrealistic Expectations:** Family Time is seldom a disappointment to children. However, parents may sometimes feel like the lesson did not go as well as they had hoped. Often this disappointment is directly related to the parent's expectations. Keep in mind that kids learn valuable things over time. You don't have to get something fantastic out of each Family Time. Be prepared to learn right along with your kids.

X **Xpect a Future:** One day your children will grow up and start families of their own. As your children raise your grandchildren they will be equipped with positive memories and effective tools to pass along the faith of their fathers.

Y **Y? Y? Y?** Questions are cool. Frederick Beuchner says, "If you want big answers then ask small questions." "What did you learn at Sunday School?" is a big question. "Who did you sit next to at Sunday School?" is a smaller question that can lead to more discussion.

Z **Zees ees Fun!** Remember the most important things you can do: take your time, engage your child, and have fun together. A silly accent never hurts either!

Family Time Format

The "Family Time Format" is a simple structure that families can use when leading a Family Time activity. You may want to tweak and modify the structure to meet the needs of your family.

Younger children benefit from using the same format from week to week. They may want to repeat the activity again and again. Remember, repetition is how young children learn. Be sure to call your time together "Family Time." When your kids are grown, you want them to look back and be able to identify times of formal spiritual training in the same way they can identify school, sports, and church.

Families of older children may want to make the lesson less formal. For example, you may not have a "Family Time Theme Song." Instead, you can invite your teens to share a favorite song. Ask them why they like the song. Is it the beat, the singer, the words?

Meet Weekly:

The goal is to lead a weekly Family Time in your home. Try to designate and reserve the same time each week, recognizing that on occasion you will need the flexibility to schedule around conflicts.

No Fuss Dinner:

Plan a simple dinner so that everyone in the family can participate. You don't want one parent spending a lot of time fixing the meal and another parent spending a lot of time cleaning up. Minimize dinner preparation and clean-up by using paper plates and paper cups. Just by looking at how the table is set, children will know it's Family Time night. You may want to use leftovers or order in dinner. Keep it simple.

Discuss the Previous Family Time:

During dinner talk about what the family did last week during Family Time. Challenge the children to try and remember the activity and message. Talk about the highlights and use this time to reinforce the message and its potential application during the past week.

You'll be surprised to learn that children will remember back two weeks, three weeks, maybe more.

Family Time Theme Song:

Pick your own family "theme song." Since this is for your spiritual training time, consider songs that talk about faith, family, relationships, and love.

Play this song after dinner and just before the evening lesson and activity. Younger children like to create a dance or hand motions to go with the song. This song signals that Family Time is here while building excitement and anticipation.

SONG IDEAS:
"The Family Prayer Song (As For Me and My House)" by Maranatha
"Creed" by Rich Mullins

Prayer:

Open the Family Time with prayer. Children and parents can take turns. Teach the children to pray about a wide variety of topics, joys, and concerns.

Message:

Decide in advance and practice the activity you will use. Communicate clearly the main principle or value being taught through the lesson.

Object Lesson:

Each Family Time has an object lesson or activity that reinforces and helps children remember the main message.

Memorize:

Repeat the short, rhyming phrase included with the lesson. The rhyme is designed to help children remember the lesson.

Prayer:

Close the time together with a prayer. Tie the prayer to the lesson. Try different methods of prayer such as holding hands and praying, pray from oldest to youngest, or say "popcorn" prayers (one- or two-word prayers about a specific topic).

Plan Ahead for Next Week:

Many lessons require that you gather specific objects or purchase items from the store. Look ahead to next week's Family Time activity to make sure you have all the necessary ingredients.

Lesson 1:
LAZARUS

 TEACHING GOAL: God gave Jesus power over death.

1. Play theme song
2. Pray
3. Lesson and discussion
4. Memorize: **Jesus cried when Lazarus died; Jesus talked and out Lazarus walked.**
5. Close in prayer

 SCRIPTURE: John 11:1-44 The story of Lazarus.

 MATERIALS: One roll of toilet paper for each person

Words that are written in **bold** are when you, the parent, are speaking. Feel free to use your own words.

Big Idea

Tell the story of Lazarus. Condense it into words your children will understand. Include the following points when you tell the story because you will be acting out the event:

- Lazarus, a friend of Jesus, was sick and died.
- He had been dead four days when Jesus came to town.
- Lazarus' sisters, Mary and Martha, said to Jesus, "Lord, if you had been here my brother would not have died."
- Jesus cried for his friend Lazarus.
- Jesus prayed and thanked God for hearing him.
- Lazarus rose from the dead.
- Lazarus came out of the tomb with strips of linen wrapped around his hands, feet, and face.

B▷ Activity

Take turns wrapping up each child in a roll of toilet paper and acting out the story. Start at the head and ask the child to turn around using short steps. As the child turns, gradually feed out the roll lower on the body until they are covered from head to toe.

Children enjoy watching parents being wrapped in the toilet paper. If younger children are afraid, then wrap up the parent. Or, do not cover the child's face, but start wrapping instead at the neck or chest.

After the child or parent is wrapped, then he or she is Lazarus as the story is acted out. One child or parent is Jesus and another can be Mary. Gently lower Lazarus to the ground. If Lazarus stands stiff and leans back then someone else can lower him to the ground. For example:

- Mary—"Jesus, if you had been here my brother Lazarus would not have died."
- Jesus—(Praying to God) "Father, thank you for hearing my prayer. Lazarus, come out!" (holding arms straight out at his side)
- Lazarus—Breaks out of the toilet paper with his arms and legs.

For older children, you may add lines about Lazarus being dead for 4 days and Jesus crying for his friend.

OPTION: If the children are comfortable being wrapped up for a few minutes, then you can add a game of hide-and-seek. The parent or child who is wrapped up must lie down waiting to hear the words, "Lazarus, come out!"

The parent/child playing Jesus goes and hides. The parent/child playing Mary must go get Jesus and bring him back to raise Lazarus by saying, "Lazarus, come out!"

▶ Application

Jesus prayed to God just like we do. Jesus cried just like we do. He was sad for his friends Martha, Mary, and Lazarus. God wants us to know that Jesus can identify with our weaknesses and that we can feel comfortable talking to him about anything that we are feeling or needing.

It's also important for us to recognize that Jesus is powerful. He is strong and able to overcome death, sickness, and other problems that we experience. We should remember to thank him regularly for loving us and taking care of us.

Lesson 2:
FRIENDS

TEACHING GOAL: Friends provide support.

1. Play theme song
2. Pray
3. Review last lesson
4. Lesson and discussion
5. Memorize: **Be a friend; support, don't bend.**
6. Close in prayer

SCRIPTURE: Exodus 17:8-13 (verse 12) "When Moses' hands grew tired, they took a stone and put it under him and he sat on it. Aaron and Hur held his hands up—one on one side, one on the other."

MATERIALS: 2 heavy books

Words that are written in **bold** are when you, the parent, are speaking. Feel free to use your own words.

Big Idea

It's important to choose good friends. Friends encourage and support us when we are feeling sad and alone. Friends can also help us make good choices, and we can do the same for our friends.

In the Old Testament, the book of Exodus, we learn that the lives of many people depended on Moses and his friends. Moses and the Israelites were in a battle against the Amalekites. The Israelites loved God and the Amalekites hated God. Moses and his friends Aaron and Hur went to the top of a hill to watch a battle. Moses had a special walking stick that he received from God. If Moses held the stick over his head, the Israelites would start winning the battle. If Moses lowered the stick, then the Israelites would start losing the battle. Moses' friends

Aaron and Hur held up Moses' arms when he got tired, and the Israelites won the battle. Thanks to the support of his friends, Moses and the Israelites were saved.

 Activity

Give each child a turn to hold two heavy books over his or her head, one in each hand. Use a clock or count out loud how many seconds the child can hold up the heavy books. Arms must be kept straight. Stop counting when any part of the arm drops below the shoulders. Give each child a second turn, but this time count how long each child can hold up the heavy books with a friend holding each arm for support. You will get tired of counting before your arms supported by friends get tired.

 Application

Friends provide support. Take turns telling about a time when a friend helped you. What can you do this week to help one of your friends?

Lesson 3:
FISHERS OF MEN

TEACHING GOAL: God wants us to share the Good News about Jesus with others.

1. Play theme song
2. Pray
3. Review last lesson
4. Lesson and discussion
5. Memorize: **I am God's fisher of men; when I share his Good News plan.**
6. Close in prayer

SCRIPTURE: Matthew 4:18-22 "As Jesus was walking beside the Sea of Galilee, he saw two brothers, Simon called Peter and his brother Andrew. They were casting a net into the lake, for they were fishermen. 'Come, follow me,' Jesus said, 'and I will make you fishers of men.' At once they left their nets and followed him. Going on from there, he saw two other brothers, James son of Zebedee and his brother John. They were in a boat with their father Zebedee, preparing their nets. Jesus called them, and immediately they left the boat and their father and followed him."

Acts 3:11-26 Peter speaks to the onlookers. He tells others the good news: repent and believe in Jesus, the Son of God, so that you will be raised up like Jesus.

Matthew 28:16-20 "Then the eleven disciples went to Galilee, to the mountain where Jesus had told them to go. When they saw him, they worshiped him; but some doubted. Then Jesus came to them and said, 'All authority in heaven and on earth has been given to me. Therefore go and make disciples of all nations, baptizing them in the name of the Father and of the Son and of the Holy Spirit, and teaching them to obey everything I have commanded you. And surely I am with you always, to the very end of the age.'"

MATERIALS: Large box
Fishing poles
Weights to put on the end of the fishing line
Buckets and rope or garden hose
Paper people or small plastic toy characters

Words that are written in **bold** are when you, the parent, are speaking. Feel free to use your own words.

 ## Big Idea

When you go fishing, what are you trying to catch? Fish. **What do you use for bait?** Worms, flies, etc.

Jesus had a group of twelve close friends. Do you know what they are called in the Bible? Disciples. **Did you know that at least four of his twelve disciples were fishermen?**

When Jesus met the four fisher-men—Peter, Andrew, James, and John—he said, "Follow me and I will make you fishers of men." What is a fisher of people trying to catch? Other people. **What bait did Peter, Andrew, James, and John use to catch other people?** The Good News: We can go to heaven by believing in Jesus, the Son of God.

Jesus commands Christians to tell others the good news (Matthew 28:16-20). **When he called his disciples to be fishers of men, it was to tell others about Jesus so that they could also go to heaven.**

Share stories of times you have shared Jesus with others.

 Activity

Do this activity outside. Put weights on the end of the fishing line instead of hooks. Use a large box as a boat. Each child takes a turn being a fisherman in the boat. Others stay far away while kids are learning to cast. Place buckets containing paper people or plastic characters close to the box-boat. When the child successfully drops the lure (weight) into the bucket, he or she may take out one of the people. Using rope or a garden hose, make circular areas farther out in the yard and place paper people or plastic characters within the circles. Each time a child casts into the area, he or she may take out one of the people. Wading pools also make great target areas.

As the children take turns playing, explain again how Jesus used the term "fishers of men" to describe our sharing the good news with family, friends, and people we meet.

 Application

Let's list the names of some people we could share Jesus with. Make a list of people and then pray for them.

Lesson 4:
INVISIBLE AND POWERFUL

 TEACHING GOAL: Even though we cannot see God, he is there and he is powerful!

1. Play theme song
2. Pray
3. Review last lesson
4. Lesson and discussion
5. Memorize: **Just like air; God is there.**
6. Close in prayer

 SCRIPTURE: John 6:46 "No one has seen the Father except the one who is from God; only he has seen the Father."

Romans 1:20 "For since the creation of the world God's invisible qualities—his eternal power and divine nature—have been clearly seen, being understood from what has been made, so that men are without excuse."

 MATERIALS: Balloon

Words that are written in **bold** are when you, the parent, are speaking. Feel free to use your own words.

A▶ Big Idea

Can you see God? No. **Can you see some of the things that God does?** Yes. **Let's list some of the ways that we know God is powerful by looking at the things he does.** He creates things, answers prayer, heals people, solves problems, etc. **All of these become evidence of God's strength and power.**

⯈ Activity

With the children standing around you, hold the empty balloon in your hands. **I'm going to count to "three" and then let this balloon go. Watch out so that it doesn't hit you! One, two, three!** Let the balloon go and it will fall to the ground. **That didn't work right! How come the balloon didn't fly around the room like I wanted it to?** Listen to their answers. You didn't put air in it.

Okay, let's try it again and this time I'll put air in the balloon. Blow up the balloon. Count to three and let it go. The balloon will fly around the room. **What made the balloon fly around?** Air. **Can you see the air?** No. Repeat several times and let the children try and catch the balloon.

When you look at a tree and see the leaves moving, what makes the leaves move? Wind. **Can you see the wind?** No.

⯈ Application

It's the same way with God. The book of John tells us that no person has ever seen God. The book of Romans says that even though God's qualities may be invisible, we can still see his power in creation around us. We can see God working in our lives, the lives of others, and creation all around us. "Just like air; God is there."

Lesson 5:
EZEKIEL

 TEACHING GOAL: The Word of God is sweet, helping us overcome stubbornness and rebelliousness.

1. Play theme song
2. Pray
3. Review last lesson
4. Lesson and discussion
5. Memorize: **When the words of God we eat; they taste like honey and are sweet.**
6. Close in prayer

 SCRIPTURE: Ezekiel 2 and 3

Ezekiel 3:1-3 "And he said to me, 'Son of man, eat what is before you, eat this scroll; then go and speak to the house of Israel.' So I opened my mouth, and he gave me the scroll to eat. Then he said to me, 'Son of man, eat this scroll I am giving you and fill your stomach with it.' So I ate it, and it tasted as sweet as honey in my mouth."

 MATERIALS: Flour tortillas for each person
Honey in a squirt bottle

 IN ADVANCE: Read and become familiar with the story of Ezekiel in chapters 2 and 3. Warm up tortillas in the microwave just enough to make them more pliable.

Words that are written in **bold** are when you, the parent, are speaking. Feel free to use your own words.

 Big Idea

Ezekiel was a man of God and a prophet. God told him he had to go to the Israelites and warn them that God was not pleased with their behavior. They were disobeying

God and being very stubborn. Delivering a message from God to tell others that they are sinning is not an easy thing to do. Telling an entire nation was even harder.

God tells Ezekiel to not be afraid of the Israelites. Why do you think he told him this? Because sometimes people get mad at us when we tell them they are doing something wrong and take their anger out on us in mean ways.

God tells Ezekiel to tell them, whether they listen or not. Imagine that I'm trying to warn someone about a flood coming but the person won't listen. How do you think I would feel?

God then tells Ezekiel to eat the scroll filled with his words. This is kind of a strange request because it's unusual to eat books. What do you think it would taste like to eat a book? Why do you think God told Ezekiel to do this? Maybe to see if he would be obedient and trust him.

Ezekiel trusted God and was obedient. We often have to step out in faith, doing something we may think is difficult before God does something completely unexpected or miraculous. What happened to the scroll when Ezekiel ate it?

It may have changed from papyrus to something edible. **What did it taste like?** It was sweet like honey.

God told Ezekiel that those he was speaking to were familiar and to not be afraid. He warned him that they wouldn't listen but to still speak to them. Why do you think God wanted Ezekiel to speak to them even though he knew they wouldn't listen to him or change? God wanted them to have the opportunity to hear the message and be warned about their behavior. They still had to make their own choice. He wanted Ezekiel to be obedient too.

 Activity

Squeeze honey onto tortillas, writing scripture verses, the name "God" or pictures with the honey.

Roll the tortilla into a scroll shape.

Eat the newly formed scroll.

Enjoy the words of God, that taste sweet as honey!

Application

We don't literally eat books, but how can we eat the Word of God in our own lives? By reading it, memorizing it, and thinking about it regularly. **Can you think of a verse or story that you know by heart?** Have child give you an example.

How can this verse or story taste sweet to you? By being obedient to what we read and letting God speak to us through it. By listening to what God has to say, we won't become stubborn and rebellious like the Israelites did.

Lesson 6:
CROSS AND TOMB

TEACHING GOAL: Jesus suffered for our sin, died, and rose again, conquering death so that we might join him in heaven.

1. Play theme song
2. Pray
3. Review last lesson
4. Lesson and discussion
5. Memorize: **Jesus rose on Easter day; he takes my sin away.**
6. Close in prayer

SCRIPTURE: Matthew 27-28; Luke 24

MATERIALS: Wood to make three crosses:
> Three 3' pieces
> Three 2' pieces
> Six large and six small nails
> Hammer
> Duct tape
> 1 box with lid, the size a case of paper comes in
> Paper, pen, crayons
> White handkerchief or washcloth

Words that are written in **bold** are when you, the parent, are speaking. Feel free to use your own words.

 Big Idea

In your own words, tell the story of Easter from Matthew 27-28 while you are making the crosses. Help your children understand the schedule of events. **Jesus had the Passover meal with his friends, the disciples, on Thursday. He was arrested Thursday night while praying in the Garden of Gethsemane. He was tried on Friday and crucified on**

Friday. On Sunday he rose from the grave. Everything happened so quickly. It was just five days earlier that he rode into Jerusalem on a donkey with people praising him and calling him "King."

B Activity

#1: (This activity can be done over several days. Consider doing Activity #1 and #2 on Good Friday. Activity #3 can be done on Saturday. The kids can find the tomb empty on Sunday morning.) Make the three crosses by nailing the 2′ piece of wood horizontally across the vertical 3′ piece of wood. Connect the pieces one foot from the top of the 3′ piece and in the middle of the 2′ piece. Let the children help make the crosses by nailing two larger nails where the pieces of wood intersect (if you use just one nail the pieces of wood will swivel around). If you are concerned about the wood splitting, then you can pre-drill small holes for the nails. This will also help younger children when nailing.

#2: Make a tomb from the box. Cut a large, slightly oval piece of cardboard from the box top. This will be the stone. Cut a hole about half the size of your "stone" in the side of the box. Turn the box upside down and this will be the tomb. **OPTIONAL:** You can color the stone and tomb using construction paper, crayons, or spray paint.

Using three pieces of paper, draw pictures of Jesus and the two thieves. Each person should be as large as an entire sheet of paper. **OPTIONAL:** You can find images on the Internet by using a search engine to find "Jesus Coloring Pages." Color Jesus and the two thieves. Tell the story of what happened. **Back in Jesus' day they would punish criminals by nailing people to a cross and letting them hang there until they died. Jesus was not a criminal. In fact, he had never sinned. He is the only one who has never sinned, yet he was hung on a cross. There were two men hung on crosses next to Jesus. These men were criminals. They were thieves. One of these men recognized that Jesus was innocent and the Son** of God. He believed in Jesus and Jesus said, "Today you will be with me in heaven." Jesus paid the price for all our sins when he died on the cross. Like the thieves we have a choice to believe Jesus. One thief believed Jesus and the other did not. The one who believed had his sins forgiven and went with Jesus to heaven. Further discussion: **Everyone has sinned. Sin is doing the wrong thing. Jesus died for those sins. What are some sins you have committed that Jesus died for? Do you believe in Jesus and believe he died for your sins?**

When you are done coloring the pictures, use the small nails and nail the pictures to the crosses. Using the duct tape, tape the crosses to the back of the "tomb" box.

Later Friday evening, take Jesus off the cross and put him in the tomb. Also, remove the thieves and put them away.

#3: Saturday night after the children go to bed, remove Jesus from the tomb. Leave the stone rolled away. When the children come down on Sunday morning, let them see Jesus out of the tomb. Retell the story and add (Luke 24) how Jesus visited with his friends, the disciples, before going up in the clouds to heaven.

 Application

The resurrection is a rich part of our faith. Take time to marvel with your kids at the tremendous sacrifice of the cross and the amazing power of the resurrection.

Lesson 7:
DORCAS HELPING OTHERS

TEACHING GOAL: The story of Dorcas teaches us the value of serving others.

1. Play theme song
2. Pray
3. Review last lesson
4. Lesson and discussion
5. Memorize: **Help those in need; with clothes, food, and good deeds.**
6. Close in prayer

SCRIPTURE: 1 Corinthians 13:4 "Love is kind."

Acts 9:36-42 "In Joppa there was a disciple named Tabitha (which, when translated, is Dorcas), who was always doing good and helping the poor. About that time she became sick and died, and her body was washed and placed in an upstairs room. Lydda was near Joppa; so when the disciples heard that Peter was in Lydda, they sent two men to him and urged him, 'Please come at once!' Peter went with them, and when he arrived he was taken upstairs to the room. All the widows stood around him, crying and showing him the robes and other clothing that Dorcas had made while she was still with them. Peter sent them all out of the room; then he got down on his knees and prayed. Turning toward the dead woman, he said, 'Tabitha, get up.' She opened her eyes, and seeing Peter she sat up."

MATERIALS: Pillowcase for each child (old or new)
Scissors
Permanent markers
Store-bought clothing

Words that are written in **bold** are when you, the parent, are speaking. Feel free to use your own words.

Big Idea

Tell the story of Dorcas. Emphasize that Dorcas was known for doing good, helping the poor, and making clothes for other people. She demonstrated love by serving and helping others. **Do we know anybody who makes or gives clothes to people who need them? What are some good things we can do to help people who need food, clothing, or a place to stay?**

Activity

Dorcas made clothes, so we are going to make a shirt. Using the pillowcase, make a nightshirt or play shirt. Locate the center of the closed end and cut a hole large enough for the head. On the sides of the pillowcase, just below the closed end seam, cut a hole on each side for the arms. Decorate the shirt using the markers. For example, use the Christian fish symbol, write the name "Dorcas" or trace the child's hands and write "helping hands."

Find a mission that accepts clothing and provides it for people in need (e.g. Salvation Army, Prison Fellowship, local children's homes, and missionaries often have clothing needs).

Take the children to a store and purchase clothing for someone in need. Have the whole family deliver or help mail the items.

Application

Generosity is a tool to give a little of our selfishness away. As children learn to help others, they are looking at their needs. One of the best ways to help someone learn to be less demanding and self-centered is to practice giving and helping others. Use this activity to teach children the value of generosity.

Lesson 8:
DAVID AND GOLIATH

 TEACHING GOAL: The story of David teaches us that God can protect us against big challenges.

1. Play theme song
2. Pray
3. Review last lesson
4. Lesson and discussion
5. Memorize: **Like David I believe; God will protect me.**
6. Close in prayer

SCRIPTURE: 1 Samuel 17 David and Goliath

 **MATERIALS:** Tape measure
Masking tape
3" x 3" piece of cloth
2 pieces of string 3' each
Small ball or wad of paper

Words that are written in **bold** are when you, the parent, are speaking. Feel free to use your own words.

Big Idea

Read the story of David and Goliath and tell it in your own words. Include how David was a shepherd boy and Goliath was a big man nine feet tall. David had a sling and five stones as his weapon. Goliath had a sword, spear, and shield. Goliath did not believe in God. David believed that God would protect him and give him the victory.

Activity

Let's measure how big Goliath was compared to how big you are. You can measure Goliath's height on a tree, the side of a house, or on the ground. Use the masking tape to mark nine feet. Be careful not to damage the tree or house when marking Goliath's height. Then measure the height of the children compared to Goliath.

Let's make a sling using a piece of cloth and two pieces of string. Cut a square piece of cloth approximately three inches by three inches. Poke a hole in each of the four corners. On one side of the square, thread a three-foot piece of string down through the bottom hole and up through the top hole. Pull the string through until the two ends meet. Repeat the process by threading a second three-foot piece of string down through the remaining bottom hole and up through the remaining top hole.

Practice! Use something soft like a small ball or a wadded-up piece of paper. Wrap two of the strings around your finger and hold the other two strings loosely between your fingers as you swing the sling around in a circle. When you let go, point your hand at the target and release the two loose strings.

You will learn how hard it is to use a sling. **It is not easy to use a sling. But God had been preparing David for years to battle Goliath. David was a shepherd boy who spent hours looking after sheep. He must have practiced using a sling over and over again until he was good** enough to scare off wolves, bears, and lions that would attack the sheep. Are you doing anything in your life over and over again that God might use in the future? Listen to answers.

Act out the story of David and Goliath. The adult can play the role of Goliath and the child play the role of David. Use an empty sling and a "pretend" stone.

> **GOLIATH: Who will come out and fight me?**

> **DAVID: I will.**

> **GOLIATH: But you are just a small boy! I have this big spear and shield. What do you have?**

> **DAVID: I have a sling, five stones, and the one true God is on my side.**

> **GOLIATH: I do not know this God of yours. I will crush you, then crush all of Israel.**

> **DAVID:** Swing the sling and let go as Goliath approaches.

> **GOLIATH:** Raise your arm like you're holding a sword as you approach David. When he lets go of the sling, act like a rock hit you on the head and fall down.

> **DAVID:** Walk up to Goliath lying on the ground and say, **My God has protected me!**

 ## Application

Just because you are small doesn't mean that you are weak. Goliath was a bully and he seemed strong on the outside. He was picking on David and the other Israelites. God wanted to teach David a valuable lesson that real strength is on the inside. David had God on his side and that is stronger than anything.

Lesson 9:
ARK OF THE COVENANT

TEACHING GOAL: God is with us.

1. Play theme song
2. Pray
3. Review last lesson
4. Lesson and discussion
5. Memorize: **God gave us the ark to say, "I am with you every day."**
6. Close in prayer

SCRIPTURE: Exodus 25:10-22 God gave Moses specific instructions for building the ark of the covenant.

Deuteronomy 10:1-5 God told Moses to put the Ten Commandments into the ark of the covenant.

Joshua 3:14-17 The ark symbolized God's presence and went before the people as they obeyed God.

1 Samuel 6:1-16 God designed the ark to be for the Israelites. When it was taken by the Philistines, the Israelites could hardly wait to get it back.

1 Kings 8:1-13 Solomon built the temple and welcomed the ark to its new home.

Revelation 11:19 In John's vision in Revelation, the ark of the covenant was in heaven.

MATERIALS: Large cardboard box (refrigerator or wardrobe)
Two broom handles
Utility knife
Gold spray paint
Bible

Words that are written in **bold** are when you, the parent, are speaking. Feel free to use your own words.

Big Idea

Describe the ark of the covenant by reading a few of the scriptures so that your family can hear about the ark. Exodus contains the directions for building the ark. Then you may choose to tell your children this summary: **God gave Moses directions to build an ark—but this ark wasn't a boat, it was a special treasure box. The ark of the covenant was a symbol of God's presence and the Israelites carried it with them for many years. They even put it in a special place of honor. The ark contained items to remind people of what God had done.**

Three items we know were in the ark of the covenant: The Ten Commandment tablets (Deuteronomy 10:2), **Aaron's staff** (Numbers 17:10), **and a jar of manna** (Exodus 16:34). **Why were these put in the ark?** So the people would remember what God had done for them.

Activity

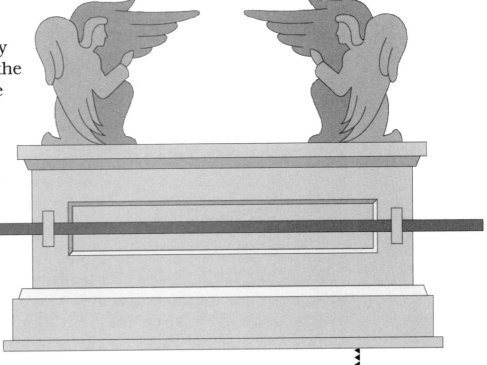

Parents use the utility knife to cut holes in the cardboard box for the broom handles to fit through. The holes should be about a third of the way from the top and two or three inches from the sides on each of the long ends of the box. Allow the children to paint the box (this may need to be done outside) and decorate it to look like a fancy gold treasure box.

While building the ark, ask your children what it might have been like for the Israelites to build their ark. **What do you think the Israelites were thinking about when they built the ark?** It cost a lot of money. God likes nice things. This box must be very special. **How heavy might the ark have been if it was made of gold?** Very. **How might the people feel who had to carry it around?** Important. Special. Tired.

When the box is complete and dry, sit around it and discuss the following questions: **Why do you think God wanted Moses to build the ark of the covenant?** To remind the Israelites of God's presence. So people wouldn't forget God. **What are ways we are reminded of God's presence today?** We learn about God at church. When we read the Bible we remember God. We talk to God when we pray.

After making the ark, ask each child to find two things in their rooms that remind them of God. They may choose a children's Bible, picture of Mom and Dad, Bible story book, or something completely different. Ask them why they chose that item and have them put it in the ark. **In the same way manna, the staff, and the Ten Commandments reminded the Israelites about what God had done, these items remind us of God.**

The Israelites carried the ark around on poles. We are going to march around the outside of the house carrying our ark.

 Application

The Israelites were easily fooled into following false gods during the time Moses was leading them. But the ark of the covenant became a visible reminder that God was with them, even when they felt alone or separated from God. When Jesus came to earth many years later, he opened up the door to a personal relationship with God—so now we know God is near because he is in our hearts.

Lesson 10:
ANGELS ARE POWERFUL

TEACHING GOAL: God's powerful angels command respect and fear.

1. Play theme song
2. Pray
3. Review last lesson
4. Lesson and discussion
5. Memorize: **We fall down to the ground; when God's angels are around.**
6. Close in prayer

SCRIPTURE: Joshua 5:14 Joshua has crossed the Jordan River and entered the Promised Land. He meets an angel of the Lord. Joshua fell facedown to the ground in reverence.

Luke 2:9-10 "An angel of the Lord appeared to them, and the glory of the Lord shone around them, and they were terrified. But the angel said to them, 'Do not be afraid.'"

Luke 1:29-30 "Mary was greatly troubled at his words and wondered what kind of greeting this might be. But the angel said to her, 'Do not be afraid.'"

Luke 1:11-13 "Then an angel of the Lord appeared to him.... When Zechariah saw him, he was startled and was gripped with fear. But the angel said to him: 'Do not be afraid.'"

MATERIALS: Large picture of powerful angel (included)
Sheet with 10 small angel images (included)
Picture or figurine of "cute" angel (included)
Markers, crayons, tape

Words that are written in **bold** are when you, the parent, are speaking. Feel free to use your own words.

Big Idea

Describe the picture that comes to your mind when you think about angels. In stores, books, and even at church we see images of angels. Often these images are very different from the angels described in the Bible.

In the Old Testament Joshua crosses over the Jordan River into the Promised Land. As he prepares to attack the city of Jericho, he meets an angel of the Lord. What does Joshua do? He falls down on his face out of respect for the angel.

In the New Testament Zechariah, the father of John the Baptist, is visited in the temple by an angel. The Bible says Zechariah was gripped with fear. The first thing the angel says is "Do not be afraid."

At the birth of Jesus, an angel appears to the shepherds. The Bible says that the shepherds were terrified at the sight of the angel. The first thing the angel says is "Do not be afraid." When an angel came to Mary to tell her she was going to have the baby Jesus, the Bible says she was troubled by the angel's message. The first thing the angel says is "Do not be afraid."

Tell me two common things about angels from these Bible stories:

1. The first impression of an angel is one of fear, terror, or respect.
2. The first thing the angel says is "Do not be afraid." It's like the angel says, "Don't worry, I'm one of the good guys."

 Activity

I'm going to show you a picture of an angel. I want to warn you that you may feel fear, terror, awe, and respect when you see this picture, but do not be afraid. This angel is one of the good guys.

From a hiding place bring out the picture of the "cute" angel. **Are you afraid?** No. **Why?** Listen to their answers. **Although this is a common picture of an angel that we will see in books and stores, it does not represent the type of angel we read about in the Bible.**

Angels in the Bible primarily serve two purposes:

1. **They are messengers delivering words from God to people.**

2. **They are warriors fighting spiritual battles against the evil one.**

There is a spiritual battle taking place between good and evil. Hold up the picture again. **Do you think this is the type of angel God has sent to protect us in the spiritual battle?**

I have never seen an angel, although I believe they are around us. Here is a picture of an angel who looks more like a warrior who will protect us. This is an angel who might generate feelings of respect, power, fear, and awe. Show the picture of the powerful angel. **If this angel were standing here, bright as a light and ten feet tall, how do you think that would make you feel?**

We are going to play a game. Here are the rules:

1. **The first one to 50 points wins.**

2. **I am going to show you either a picture of the "cute" angel or a picture of the powerful angel. If I show you the picture of a powerful angel, then the first one to drop to the floor gets five points. If I show you the picture of a "cute" angel and you drop to the floor, then you lose five points. Like Joshua, we are going to show respect for the powerful angel by dropping to the floor.**

3. Have the players stand side by side, with some space in between. Turn your back to the players. Arrange to show one of the two angel pictures, then turn around quickly. If it is the powerful angel, then give five points to the first player to drop to the floor. If it is the cute angel then take away five points from any player whose hands touch the floor.

4. Players may want to repeat the game.

Give each child a copy of the large angel. While they are coloring it, talk about what they have learned about angels in the Bible. Give each adult a page of ten smaller angels to color.

 ## Application

You may not know this but sometimes at night when you are sleeping I come into your room and say a prayer over you. I ask God to keep you safe, healthy, and to draw you closer to him. You do not see when I come in and pray for you; we do not see the angels that are around us. God sends his angels to protect us. This next week, when I come in and pray for you at night, I am going to tape an angel somewhere in your room. It will remind you that I am praying for you and that God's angels are all around us.

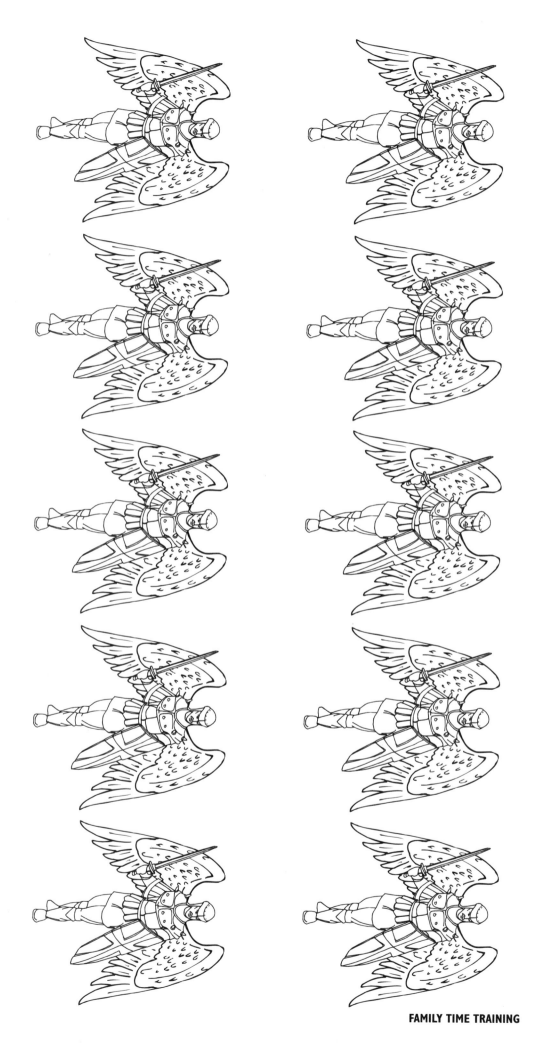

46

Lesson 11:
DANIEL IN THE LIONS' DEN

TEACHING GOAL: Daniel obeyed and trusted in God and God protected him.

1. Play theme song
2. Pray
3. Review last lesson
4. Lesson and discussion
5. Memorize: Younger—**When I'm afraid I'm going to pray.**
   Older—**When the hungry lions growled and roared, Daniel put his faith and trust in the Lord.**
6. Close in prayer

SCRIPTURE: Daniel 6 Daniel and the Lions' Den

MATERIALS: 15 copies of the lion's head on orange paper
Pink or white construction paper (10 sheets)
Clear packing tape
A blindfold (an adult winter cap pulled down over the children's eyes works)
A treat/reward for each child

IN ADVANCE: Cut fifteen hand prints out of white or pink construction paper to be used later.

Words that are written in **bold** are when you, the parent, are speaking. Feel free to use your own words.

A▶ Big Idea

As you work through this lesson, take time to talk about how God protects us. Read the story of Daniel in the lions' den up to the point in which they throw Daniel in the den and roll the stone over the den for the night.

B▶ Activity

Have the children cut out the lions' heads. You will need a total of approximately fifteen heads. As the kids are making the lions, remind them how dangerous, strong, and ferocious lions are—suggesting that they have a loud roar because they can open their mouths so wide.

Once the heads are cut out, take pieces of packing tape and attach the ends so that the sticky side is on the outside—like you would use to stick a poster to the wall. Make the tape ovals big enough to cover the mouths of the lions and hard to miss when kids step on them. Put these tape rolls over the lions' mouths so that their open mouths are ready to "grab" anyone who happens to walk their way.

Next, identify a two- or three-foot wide path in a room. You may want to use furniture to create boundaries to mark the path. This path is the lions' den. Place the lion heads on the floor in the "den." The goal is to have at least one of the lions stick to each child as they "walk through their night in the lions' den" (have the children keep their socks on as it will help the lions stick). Be sure that the den is well saturated with lions.

Have family members stand in a line at one end of the den and, one at a time, each person will walk through the lions. If the tape from a lion's mouth sticks to a sock, that represents being eaten by the lion. Daniel was in the dark so we are going to blindfold you before you walk through the den. (If younger children are nervous about being blindfolded then you can have them close their eyes.) The other family members will be watching, so after you blindfold the next player, move the lion heads around. It's important that everyone has at least one lion head stuck to their sock.

The lights may be turned off and/or parents and siblings can growl like the lions to add to the effect as each child negotiates the lions' den. If a child is nearing the end with no lion in tow, parents need to move the lions to ensure the last steps serve up dinner for one of the lions. Reset the den for each child to ensure adequate lion saturation.

After each child has had a turn getting gobbled up, tell them they get one more chance to make it through the den without getting gobbled up to get their treat/reward, but they need to wait out of sight in another room while you "reset" the den. While the kids are out, reset the den by placing the "hands of God" you made in advance over the mouths of each of the lions. Make sure that the hand completely covers the tape.

One at a time, bring the kids to the entrance of the den already blindfolded. This time, however, before they start their walk, have them say the following prayer:

> **"Dear God,**
> **No matter what is ahead of me,**
> **I know you can protect me. Amen."**

As they make it to the end of the den unscathed, remove their blindfold and give them God's reward for their trust and faith in him. Repeat for each child.

When all the children have made it through the den, pick up and complete the story of Daniel and the lions' den from where you left off earlier in the evening. Be sure to emphasize how the hands of God that protected Daniel are there to protect them too.

 **Application**

End by emphasizing the following three points:
> **Daniel loved and obeyed God.**
> **Daniel trusted God.**
> **God loved and protected Daniel.**

Lesson 12:
CAIN

 TEACHING GOAL: Stop sin early before it leads to more sin.

1. Play theme song
2. Pray
3. Review last lesson
4. Lesson and discussion
5. Memorize: **When your sin grows; you'd better run before it blows.**
6. Close in prayer

 SCRIPTURE: Genesis 4:1-15 Story of Cain and the progression of his sin.

James 4:7-8a "Resist the devil, and he will flee from you. Come near to God and he will come near to you."

 **MATERIALS:** Balloon, marker, safety pin

IN ADVANCE: Write the word "SIN" in big letters with a marker on a deflated balloon.

Words that are written in **bold** are when you, the parent, are speaking. Feel free to use your own words.

Ⓐ Big Idea

Tell the story of Cain and Abel and discuss how Cain started out with one sin—not giving his best—and let it grow to anger, and then jealousy, and then hurting his brother. **How did Cain's sin continue to grow? What did he do to make it worse? What warning did God give him regarding his sin(s)?** Genesis 4:7 "If you do what is right, will you not be accepted? But if you do not do what is right, sin is crouching at your door; it desires to have you, but you must master it."

Activity

Put a little air into the balloon. **Watch Cain's sin grow and grow! The air in the balloon represents his first sin—not giving God his best.**

Blow more air into the balloon. **When God corrected Cain for not giving his best, Cain sinned again by getting angry.** Blow more air into the balloon. **After getting angry, Cain sinned again by becoming jealous of his brother.** Blow more air into the balloon. The balloon should be full to the bursting point. **Finally, Cain got so mad that he hit and hurt his brother. Cain allowed sin to grow and grow in his life.**

This balloon could explode just like Cain's anger! Walk toward one of the children holding the balloon out in front of you. The child should naturally pull back. **See how** (name of child) **pulled back! That is exactly what we need to do when we see sin our lives. We need to flee and get away from sin.**

How could Cain have handled his sin differently? After not bringing his best to God, Cain could have said he was sorry. This would keep his sin from growing into anger, jealousy, and hurting others. Let the air out of the balloon. **Deal with sin immediately so it doesn't blow up.**

Application

In the days ahead, when confronting sin (lying, steeling, whining, greed) say, **I hope you don't let your sin grow and explode like the balloon!**

Lesson 13:
BUILDERS

TEACHING GOAL: Our motive for doing anything and everything needs to be from God.

1. Play theme song
2. Pray
3. Review last lesson
4. Lesson and discussion
5. Memorize: **The "babblers" couldn't build a tower; but the wall was built with God's power.**
6. Close in prayer

SCRIPTURE: Genesis 11:3-4 "They said to each other, 'Come, let's make bricks and bake them thoroughly.' They used brick instead of stone, and tar for mortar. Then they said, 'Come, let us build ourselves a city, with a tower that reaches to the heavens, so that we may make a name for ourselves and not be scattered over the face of the whole earth.'"

Nehemiah 2:12 God put in Nehemiah's heart the desire to rebuild the wall for Jerusalem.

Nehemiah 2:20 "The God of heaven will give us success. We his servants will start rebuilding."

Nehemiah 4:6 "So we rebuilt the wall till all of it reached half its height, for the people worked with all their heart."

Nehemiah 6:15-16 "So the wall was completed on the twenty-fifth of Elul, in fifty-two days. When all our enemies heard about this, all the surrounding nations were afraid and lost their self-confidence, because they realized that this work had been done with the help of our God."

MATERIALS: Bag of small marshmallows
(2 bags for larger groups)
Box of toothpicks (2 for larger groups)

Words that are written in **bold** are when you, the parent, are speaking. Feel free to use your own words.

A▶ Big Idea

We are going to talk about builders. Who do we know that is a builder? What do they build?

The following is a summary of the story of the Tower of Babel. Feel free to put it into your own words. **In the book of Genesis, a group of people decided to build a tall tower called the Tower of Babel. Listen to part of the story:**

"Come, let us build ourselves a city, with a tower that reaches to the heavens, so that we may make a name for ourselves and not be scattered over the face of the whole earth." Who wanted to build this tower? The people. **Why did they want to build the tower?** To make a name for themselves (to feel important) and not to be scattered (control).

The Lord came down from heaven and the Bible says, "The LORD scattered them from there over all the earth, and they stopped building the city." (Genesis 11:8)

Did God want the tower to be built? No. **Was the tower built?** No. **In the story of the Tower of Babel, who was really important and in control?** God.

The second story is about Nehemiah. Did you know there is a whole book in the Bible containing a story about building a wall around the city of Jerusalem? Nehemiah was the builder. Why would you build a wall around a city? It provides protection and adds to the beauty of the city. **What would happen if that wall were broken?** It makes the city vulnerable (unsafe) and it looks bad.

Listen to what the Bible says about building the wall: God put it on Nehemiah's heart to build the wall around Jerusalem. Nehemiah said that God would give them success. The people worked very hard with all of their hearts. Jerusalem was known as God's city, and God would be feared and honored by other nations when the wall was rebuilt. And the wall was completed in fifty-two days. Who wanted the wall built? God.

Who wanted the wall built? God. **Was the wall built?** Yes. **Why was it important for the wall to be built?** It communicated an image of God to others.

Whatever we do—building, playing, eating, sleeping, school, or church—we need to do what God wants, not just what we want.

B Activity

Using the marshmallows and toothpicks we are going to see who can build the tallest tower. You must use a flat surface, not lean the tower against anything, and only three marshmallows and three toothpicks can be touching the bottom. Use only marshmallows and toothpicks! Ready? Go!

OPTIONAL: Work together as a group to see how tall you can make a tower. Just like the Tower of Babel, all marshmallow towers will eventually fall down.

Using the marshmallows and toothpicks, build small houses and a fence to go around the city of houses. It works best if everyone helps with the fence. The fence takes the longest time to build and just like in the story of Nehemiah, everyone works together.

 Application

Discuss which structure lasted longest and how this activity compares with the Bible lesson. **Each of us are building our lives. We can do it our own way and things don't work out. Bad things happen and we can get discouraged because the things we try to do don't work. Instead we need to listen to God and obey him. As we build our lives focused on God, good things happen and we are blessed.**

Lesson 14:
BUBBLES AND BALLOONS

TEACHING GOAL: We want to spend time and energy on things that will last forever.

1. Play theme song
2. Pray
3. Review last lesson
4. Lesson and discussion
5. Memorize: **The wind blows bubbles away; but deeds for God forever stay.**
6. Close in prayer

SCRIPTURE: Ecclesiastes 2:10-11 "I denied myself nothing my eyes desired; I refused my heart no pleasure. My heart took delight in all my work, and this was the reward for all my labor. Yet when I surveyed all that my hands had done and what I had toiled to achieve, everything was meaningless, a chasing after the wind; nothing was gained under the sun."

Ecclesiastes 1:14 "I have seen all the things that are done under the sun; all of them are meaningless, a chasing after the wind."

Matthew 6:19-21 "Do not store up for yourselves treasures on earth, where moth and rust destroy, and where thieves break in and steal. But store up for yourselves treasures in heaven, where moth and rust do not destroy, and where thieves do not break in and steal. For where your treasure is, there your heart will be also."

Matthew 19:21 "Give to the poor, and you will have treasure in heaven."

Matthew 5:44 "Love your enemies and pray for those who persecute you."

Matthew 5:3-10 The Beatitudes

Matthew 10:30 "Even the very hairs of your head are all numbered."

MATERIALS: Balloons
Bubbles
Masking tape
Permanent marker
Paper for making a list
Name tags

HINT TO PARENTS: We recommend waiting to blow up the balloons until you are ready to use them or they will be a distraction to the children.

Words that are written in **bold** are when you, the parent, are speaking. Feel free to use your own words.

 Big Idea

God is interested in details. "Even the very hairs of your head are all numbered" (Matthew 10:30). **We need to examine everything in light of God's Word to see if what we are doing draws us closer to God or moves us away from God.**

Let's make two lists of the things we have done in the past four days. One list includes things that moved us closer to God and the other list includes things that moved us away from God.

 Activity

Using a marker, write things that move you closer to God on masking tape and stick them on inflated balloons. Write on masking tape the things that moved you away from God and stick those pieces of tape on the bottle of bubbles.

Divide into teams of two. One person wears a name tag labeled "earth" and the other wears a name tag labeled "heaven." Designate a small three-foot gap on the floor. The child representing "heaven" faces the child representing "earth" on the other side of the gap. The younger the children the closer they will need to stand so that the balloon can make it easily across the gap. The person who is "earth" throws "heaven" a balloon representing an action that will last in eternity. Then earth blows bubbles and "heaven" tries to catch them but they all pop. At the end of the activity, only the balloons are in "heaven" because the bubbles popped.

OPTIONAL: Add a fan or do the activity outside.

Application

In the days ahead ask yourself, "Am I spending my time, my resources, and my energy on balloons or bubbles?"

This activity helps children evaluate their everyday choices. Sometimes children come to accept as normal the things that aren't best for their lives. Asking the right questions can go a long way to raise the awareness level of the value of certain choices children make.

Lesson 15:
SIN—MISSING THE TARGET

 TEACHING GOAL: Everyone sins and falls short of God's perfect standards.

1. Play theme song
2. Pray
3. Review last lesson
4. Lesson and discussion
5. Memorize: **Hit God's target and win; to miss his target is sin.**
6. Close in prayer

 SCRIPTURE: Romans 3:23-24 "For all have sinned and fall short of the glory of God, and are justified freely by his grace through the redemption that came by Christ Jesus."

 MATERIALS: Toothpicks, paper, and pen
Masking tape
ACTIVITY OPTION #1: Wadded-up paper and an empty trash can
ACTIVITY OPTION #2: Basketball and a hoop
ACTIVITY OPTION #3: Golf putter, golf ball, and hole
ACTIVITY OPTION #4: Ball and a target

 IN ADVANCE: Make small paper flags using the toothpicks and paper. Write on each paper flag a sin with which your children struggle. For example:

Greedy	Lazy	Bad Words	Unloving
Hitting	Lying	Selfishness	Pride
Fighting	Rudeness	Meanness	
Stealing	Disobeying Rules		

Write on pieces of masking tape attitudes, behaviors, and actions that God commands us to include in our lives:

Loving	Generous	Sharing	Serving
Humble	Pray	Peacemaker	Worship
Caring	Kind words	Compassion	Read the Bible
Tell others about Jesus			

Words that are written in **bold** are when you, the parent, are speaking. Feel free to use your own words.

 Big Idea

What are some things that all of us have in common? A heartbeat. We all live on earth. We all breathe air. **Here is one more thing all of us have in common—the Bible says we are all sinners. Everyone you know has sinned—Dad, Mom, the pastor—everyone has sinned.**

The word "sin" means "to miss the mark." Pick an activity option and use an example from that activity. This example uses a ball and target. **Imagine that the target represents the way God wants us to live—having the right attitude, using the right words, and doing the right things. This ball represents how I choose to live. When I choose to follow God's plan and have the right attitude, it is like hitting the target with the ball. But when I choose to follow my own way instead of God's way, then that is like throwing this ball and missing the target.**

Where do we learn about God's target—how God wants us to live? Reading the Bible. Listening to preachers or teachers who are teaching from the Bible. God's Spirit.

I have written some attitudes, behaviors, and actions from the Bible on these pieces of masking tape. Can you think of some others? You can write additional examples on extra pieces of masking tape.

Can you give an example of a time when you missed God's target—sin—and did something your way and not God's way? Fighting with my brother/sister instead of asking a parent for help. Breaking a dish and trying to hide it instead of telling a parent. Stealing gum from Mom's purse instead of asking for permission.

I have written examples of sins that I have seen in our family on these flags. Can you think of some other sins? You can write additional examples on extra flags.

Activity

(Consider doing this activity outside where you can stick the flags in the ground. This example is the target and ball. Adapt to whatever activity option you choose.) **We are going to try and hit the target. Tell me, what does the target represent?** God's will for our attitude, behavior, and actions. **What does the ball represent?** Our attitude, behavior, and actions. **Sometimes we do what God wants, that is hitting the target, and sometimes we choose what we want instead of what God wants, and that is like missing the target.**

We will take turns throwing at the target. If you hit the target, everyone cheers. Then take a piece of masking tape and put it on the target and read what is written on the tape. If you miss the target, then everyone yells "sin!" Take a flag, put it where you missed, and read what is written on the flag. Give everyone a turn. Stand close enough so

everyone has an opportunity to hit the target, and then move far enough away so everyone has an opportunity to miss the target.

Repeat the lesson later in the week using a different activity like golf, soccer, basketball, etc.

 Application

God wants us to be successful in life. That's like hitting the target. Unfortunately, sometimes we do the wrong things by sinning and we miss that target. Life gets messed up and we aren't successful. This week look at your actions and choose to do things that are pleasing to God.

 # Lesson 16:
SAMSON

TEACHING GOAL: God is the source of our strength.

1. Play theme song
2. Pray
3. Review last lesson
4. Lesson and discussion
5. Memorize: **Our strength from God will stay; when God we choose to obey.**
6. Close in prayer

 SCRIPTURE: Judges 13-16 The story of Samson is one of encouragement when he obeys, but disappointment when he doesn't.

 MATERIALS: Large sweatshirts
Balloons
Wigs or mops for hair
Empty boxes
Blindfolds
Children's Bible
Glow sticks
Shoestrings or rope
Camera (if available)

Words that are written in **bold** are when you, the parent, are speaking. Feel free to use your own words.

 **Big Idea**

Tell the story of Samson, covering these main points: Samson was called by God. He was a Nazirite and the strongest man on earth. God told Samson not to cut his hair. Samson fought and killed a lion. He caught 300 foxes and used them to destroy the Philistines' crops. He fought 1,000 Philistines. Then Samson is tricked by Delilah, and his hair is cut. God takes away his strength. The Philistines blind him and put him in prison. Samson is brought out of prison, and God grants him strength again. Samson pulls down the pillars, killing many Philistines.

 Activity

Put large sweatshirts on the kids. Fill them with balloons, so that they look like muscle men. Put wigs on their heads for Samson's long hair. Take a picture of each child. Make two pillars out of empty boxes (nine feet high). Blindfold the kids and have them knock down the pillars.

After dark, tie shoestrings or rope from the back of the kids. Clip on glow sticks that will come off when pulled. Chase the kids around the yard, reenacting the foxes running through the crops.

C Application

God gives us strength, but we must obey him to receive it. If you obey God, you'll be able to show that strength in various ways. You'll be able to remain calm under pressure. That requires strength. You'll be kind even when others are mean. That is strength. Look for ways this week to be strong on the inside and obey God.

Lesson 17:
LOT AND ABRAHAM

TEACHING GOAL: The story of Abraham teaches us to choose friends who follow God.

1. Play theme song
2. Pray
3. Review last lesson
4. Lesson and discussion
5. Memorize: **Lot chose friends with bad behavior; Abraham chose good friends and lived in God's favor.**
6. Close in prayer

SCRIPTURE: Genesis 11:27 to Genesis 19 The story of Lot and Abraham

Genesis 13:10-13 "Lot looked up and saw that the whole plain of the Jordan was well watered, like the garden of the Lord, like the land of Egypt, toward Zoar. (This was before the Lord destroyed Sodom and Gomorrah.) So Lot chose for himself the whole plain of the Jordan and set out toward the east.... Now the men of Sodom were wicked and were sinning greatly against the Lord."

Genesis 13:18 "So Abram moved his tents and went to live near the great trees of Mamre at Hebron, where he built an altar to the Lord."

MATERIALS: Large paper and markers
Paper towel
Clear cup with water
Food coloring
Map of the Middle East (included)

Words that are written in **bold** are when you, the parent, are speaking. Feel free to use your own words.

A Big Idea

God changed the names of Abraham and his wife Sarah. God changed Abram to Abraham and Sarai to Sarah. Do you have a nickname?

Today we're going to learn more about Abraham and Lot. Abraham was a man who served God. Lot sometimes hung around with people who tempted him to do the wrong things.

B Activity

Looking at the map of the Middle East (provided), tell the story of Abraham moving to Canaan. Pronounce the names of cities and people and ask the kids to repeat them. **Abraham was born in Ur. He moved to Haran. The Lord told Abraham, his wife Sarah and his nephew Lot to move to Canaan. They arrived in Canaan, but a drought caused them to go to Egypt for awhile. Who else do you know that lived in Egypt?** Pharaoh and Moses. **Then they moved back to Canaan.**

When they arrived in Canaan, Lot and his men were quarreling with Abraham and his men. Draw on your map a picture of a hill with Abraham and Lot on the top. **Abraham said it is not good to be fighting. He told Lot to choose whatever land he wanted and he could have it. Abraham went the other way with his family.**

Draw a city wall with people on the city wall on one side of the hill. **Lot chooses to go and live in an area called Sodom and Gomorrah where the people did the wrong things. They were sinning in lots of ways. Abraham chose to go the other way and built an altar to honor God.**

If you choose to be around people who sin and do the wrong things, you will start to sin and do wrong too. If you choose to be around people who do right, who try not to sin, you will do what's right too. Put about one inch of water in a clear cup and add 10-15 drops of food coloring and stir. Cut one-inch-wide strips of absorbent paper towel for each person. Have each person write their name on the paper towel, fold over one end, and place the other end in the colored liquid with the folded end hanging on the cup edge. Watch how the colored liquid starts to move up the strip of towel.

Lay another piece of towel away from the cup of colored liquid. **Why does the paper towel that is away from the cup not change color?** Because it is not touching the liquid. **What is happening to the paper towel that is touching the liquid?** It is soaking up the color.

 ## Application

In the same way, when we spend lots of time with people who sin and do the wrong things, then we may start doing wrong, also. But if we spend time with people who love God, then our lives will be influenced, and we will do right more often.

Notice that the longer the paper towel touches the colored liquid, the more color is soaked into the towel. The more time we spend with people who do wrong or right, the more our lives will reflect the same thing.

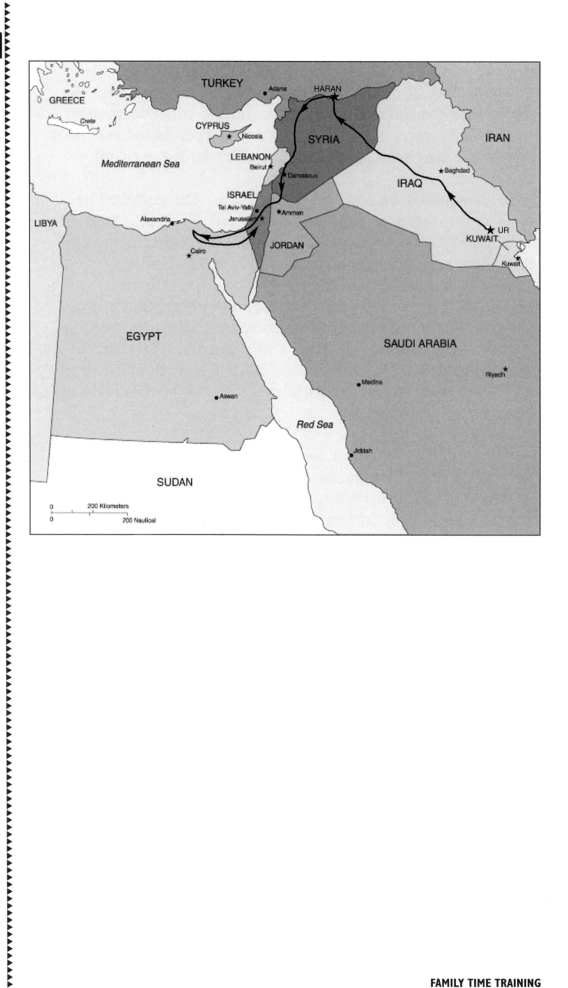

Lesson 18:
THE OATMEAL PLAGUE

 TEACHING GOAL: When facing difficult circumstances, trust God instead of complaining.

1. Play theme song
2. Pray
3. Review last lesson
4. Lesson and discussion
5. Memorize: **"Do everything without complaining or arguing." —Philippians 2:14**
6. Close in prayer

 SCRIPTURE: Numbers 14:1-38 The Israelites are in a position to leave the sparse wilderness and cross into the abundant promised land. God has promised to give them the land, but the Israelites do not trust God and begin to grumble and complain. Joshua and Caleb trust God to give them the new land, so their lives are spared and they are allowed to enter the Promised Land. The other 10 men who were "responsible for spreading the bad report" (verse 37) and started the complaining were struck down with a plague.

Numbers 13 and 14 Exploring Canaan; the people rebel

Philippians 2:14 "Do everything without complaining or arguing."

 MATERIALS: Cold, cooked oatmeal
Wet wipes (write the word "Grace" on the package)

 IN ADVANCE: Read Numbers 13 and 14. Put the story of the 12 "explorers" who were sent into the Promised Land, Canaan, into your own words, appropriate to the ages of the children present.

Words that are written in **bold** are when you, the parent, are speaking. Feel free to use your own words.

A ▶ Big Idea

Tell the story of the 12 explorers. Include the report of the 10 and the report of Joshua and Caleb. Emphasize that the people responded by complaining instead of trusting God in difficult circumstances.

God wanted the people to do something that they didn't want to do. Do your parents ever ask you to do things you don't want to do? Clean my room, chores, homework. **How do you respond?** Complain, argue, whine, or I do what my parents say.

The Bible tells us that God is slow to anger, but that the Israelites complained so much that God became angry. Have you ever complained so much that your parents became angry? There are negative consequences to our complaining. Parents might put you in a time-out or a Break, or you might lose a privilege.

The Israelites complained so much that the consequence was severe. God said he was going to give everyone a plague except those who trusted him like Joshua and Caleb. What is a plague? When the water turns to blood, when a lot of people get sick with the same thing. **Plagues are anything bad that happens to a whole group of people. Often a sickness that nearly everyone gets is referred to as a plague.**

 **Activity**

Get out the cold oatmeal and stir it in front of the kids. **We are going to take turns telling about a time when we complained or argued. When you complain, I am going to put a glob of this sticky cold oatmeal on your arm to represent the plague—we'll call it the oatmeal plague. Put your arm out onto the table in front of you.** Allow children to share. Place a glob of oatmeal on the child's arm. **This oatmeal reminds us that there are consequences when we complain. It also represents how yucky it is to complain—it is yucky to God, to our parents, to others around us, and it often feels yucky even inside of you.** (Although this is very simple, kids love it!)

After each child shares 3 times of complaining, bring out the box of wet wipes. **Moses prayed to God to forgive the people for their complaining. God heard Moses' prayer and took the plague away except for the 10 explorers who spread the bad report.** Wipe away half of the oatmeal plague with the wet wipe. **This wipe represents God's grace. God doesn't always give us what we deserve. The Israelites deserved the plague for their arguing and complaining, but God took it away.**

Jesus is part of God's plan for grace in our lives. Complaining is a sin. When we ask Jesus to forgive us for any sin, even complaining, he does. Let's each ask Jesus to forgive us for our complaining, and then I'll wipe away the remaining oatmeal to represent God's forgiveness.

 Application

Let's be more like Joshua and Caleb and trust God and our parents and do our best not to complain.

Lesson 19:
SHINE THE LIGHT OF JESUS

 TEACHING GOAL: Jesus is the light that we can reflect to others.

1. Play theme song
2. Pray
3. Review last lesson
4. Lesson and discussion
5. Memorize: **It's right; to reflect Jesus the light.**
6. Close in prayer

 SCRIPTURE: John 1:9 "The true light that gives light to every man was coming into the world."

Matthew 5:16 "Let your light shine before men, that they may see your good deeds and praise your Father in heaven."

 MATERIALS: Small flashlight
Small hand-held mirror
Pictures of friends, neighbors, missionaries, and people from other countries
A darkened room
Masking tape

Words that are written in **bold** are when you, the parent, are speaking. Feel free to use your own words.

Big Idea

Read the short scriptures listed above from your Bible (let the children see you reading the Bible). To keep their attention, have them count how many times you say the word light.

74

And, you can ask them to count how many times you say light in the two verses.

What does it mean that Jesus is the light? How does light represent Jesus? Jesus helps us see. He provides safety from falling. He creates a happy feeling and comfort.

What does it mean to say we are to shine the light of Jesus? How do others see Jesus' light when they look at us? (Do not worry if the children have unclear answers, because this lesson will help show how we shine the light of Jesus to others.)

Which of these choices represents light:
- **Hugs or hitting?**
- **Words that tear down or words that build up?**
- **Helping others or walking away from a friend who needs help?**
- **Prayer or ignoring God?**

 **Activity**

With the lights on, go into the room that will eventually be dark. Tape the pictures of family, friends, missionaries, classmates, and mission recipients on the wall. Let the children help, and make sure the pictures are spread around the room.

Write "Jesus" on a piece of masking tape or have the kids write "Jesus," and put the masking tape on the flashlight. Each child takes a turn and, one at a time, writes his or her name on masking tape and puts it on the back of a small hand-held mirror.

Demonstrate how the mirror reflects the light from the small flashlight. Show how to move the mirror to move the reflection around. Give each child a chance to move the reflection. **The flashlight represents Jesus who is the light. The**

mirror represents us. We are not the light, but we can reflect the light.

Reflect the light and move the reflection to hit each of the pictures taped around on the walls.

 Application

Ask the children if they can think about things they are able to do that shine Jesus' light to the people in the pictures.

Finish by taking turns moving the reflection to hit each member of the family: "Dad reflects Jesus to Mom, son, and daughter. Daughter reflects Jesus to Mom, Dad, and brother."

Lesson 20:
GOOD AND BAD WORDS

TEACHING GOAL: God wants us to use good words.

1. Play theme song
2. Pray
3. Review last lesson
4. Lesson and discussion
5. Memorize: **Encourage one another; build each other up.**
6. Close in prayer

SCRIPTURE: Proverbs 12:18 "Reckless words pierce like a sword, but the tongue of the wise brings healing."

Proverbs 25:18 "Like a club or a sword or a sharp arrow is the man who gives false testimony against his neighbor."

Proverbs 15:4 "The tongue that brings healing is a tree of life, but a deceitful tongue crushes the spirit."

1 Thessalonians 5:11 "Encourage one another and build each other up, just as in fact you are doing."

MATERIALS: OPTION 1: Legos or building blocks
OPTION 2: Large flip-chart-size paper, tape, and marker
Paper and pen
2 hats or 2 bowls

IN ADVANCE: Cut slips of paper approximately 2″ by 4″. For Option 1 build the shape of a person out of the Lego blocks.

Words that are written in **bold** are when you, the parent, are speaking. Feel free to use your own words.

A Big Idea

What do you think the Bible means when it says, "Words can cut like a sword." Listen to their answers. **What do you think the Bible means when it says, "Kind words can bring healing."** Listen to their answers. **There are good words and bad words. We are going to see how words can build people up and how words can tear people down.**

First, let's write on these slips of paper good words that build people up. And then we will write words that tear people down. NOTE: Children don't have to know how to read or write. Parents can do all of the reading and writing.

Building up words (include words used by members of your family).

I'll share with you	Thank you	Let's play
What's your name?	I like you	Let's work it out
I forgive you	Please	You're special
I will be your friend	Good job	Praise God
Can I help you?		

Tearing down words (include words used by members of your family when they get upset).

You're not my friend	Clumsy	You're mean
I don't like you	Idiot	Dumb
I won't do what you say	Ugly	Stupid

Put the building up words in one hat or bowl and the tearing down words in a second hat or bowl.

B Activity

OPTION 1—Bring out the Lego person. Children take turns pulling words out of the hat or bowl filled with negative words. Read the word and ask, **"Is that a building up word or tearing down word?"** Tearing down word. With each negative word take a block off the Lego person. **The words are tearing the person down.**

Repeat the activity using the hat or bowl with building up words and build the Lego person back up.

OPTION 2—Using the marker, trace each child on a large piece of flip-chart-size paper. Tape the body outline onto the wall. **CAUTION:** Be careful to use a marker that will not bleed through the paper and onto the floor. Use tape that will not pull off the paint or wallpaper.

Children take turns pulling words out of the hat or bowl filled with negative words. Read the word and ask, **"Is that a building up word or tearing down word?"** Tearing down word. With each negative word tear a piece of paper off the outline taped to the wall. **The words are tearing the person down.**

Repeat the activity using the hat or bowl with building up words and tape the torn pieces of paper back onto the child's outline.

God wants us to use words that build others up, not words that tear others down. Even when we taped the pieces back together you can still see the tears. We can use building up words like "I'm sorry" but part of the damage remains.

 Application

This week let's practice using building up words. We will point out building up words and tearing down words.

Lesson 21:
THE EXPANDING EGG

 TEACHING GOAL: A heart that is soft and open toward God will grow.

1. Play theme song
2. Pray
3. Review last lesson
4. Lesson and discussion
5. Memorize: **When our heart isn't hard; our faith will grow large.**
6. Close in prayer

 SCRIPTURE: Acts 7:58, 8:1-3, 9:1-22 The story of Paul from when his heart was hardened to when he grew in the Lord.

 MATERIALS: Uncooked egg (in its shell)
Large clear glass (allows room for the egg to grow)
Distilled white vinegar—enough to cover the egg while in the glass

 IN ADVANCE: One full day before the activity, have your child place the egg in the glass. Draw attention to the size and hardness of the shell. Cover the egg with vinegar and let the glass sit.

Words that are written in **bold** are when you, the parent, are speaking. Feel free to use your own words.

 Big Idea

Read Acts 7:58, 8:1-3, 9:1-22 or in your own words tell the story of Saul/Paul, stressing the following points:

- Saul hated the early Christians, even giving his consent for the stoning of Stephen.

- Saul wanted to go to Damascus to persecute the Christians there.
- Jesus came as a bright light and spoke to Saul on the way to Damascus, and he was converted.
- Saul, now Paul, immediately began to preach about Christ and the people were amazed.
- Acts 9:22 says, "Yet Saul **grew more and more** powerful and baffled the Jews living in Damascus by proving that Jesus is the Christ."

 Activity

Get the egg and vinegar mixture. Carefully lift out the egg using a spoon. Have the children examine the changes in the egg. By now the hard shell has dissolved and the egg has grown at least 50% bigger. (It will be covered in a translucent film, that will make the egg fragile and slippery.) **What has happened to our egg?** The shell is gone and it's bigger. **What do you think changed the egg?** The vinegar. **How is this egg like the story of Paul?** Paul had a hard heart just like the egg had a hard shell.

 Application

The egg represents a person. In this story, that person is Saul. The shell represents a hard heart. The vinegar represents Jesus. When Saul met Jesus on the road to Damascus, his hard heart went away. Each day, Saul's faith and belief in Jesus grew bigger and bigger. Jesus changed his name from Saul to Paul and gave him the special job of telling others about Jesus. You and I know about Jesus because of Paul. Jesus wants to soften our hearts too so our faith will grow.

Lesson 22:
EASTER CALENDAR

 TEACHING GOAL: We want to remember the events of Holy Week—Palm Sunday to Easter.

1. Play theme song
2. Pray
3. Review last lesson
4. Lesson and discussion
5. Memorize: **The Easter story reminds me; Jesus died and rose so I can be free.**
6. Close in prayer

 SCRIPTURE: Luke 19:28 to 24:12 8 Days, Palm Sunday to the Resurrection.

 MATERIALS: Crayons or markers
Construction paper (white, green, brown, black, yellow)
Scissors, glue
Bread, small paper cup or communion cup
Popsicle sticks
Pipe cleaner, pennies
Small pieces of cloth
Strips of paper

 IN ADVANCE: Read the events of Holy Week in Luke chapters 19-24. Each day during the week between Palm Sunday and Easter, you will be adding items to your Easter Calendar. Be prepared to read or put into your own words the events being remembered on each day.

NOTE: Begin this activity on or around Palm Sunday. Prepare the materials that will be used in creating your Easter Calendar during Family Time, and then add the items to the calendar each day during the week between Palm Sunday and Easter.

Words that are written in **bold** are when you, the parent, are speaking. Feel free to use your own words.

 Big Idea

It is amazing how many events took place in Jesus' life during the week between Palm Sunday and Easter. In just one week, people changed their minds from wanting to crown Jesus as king to wanting Jesus killed, crucified. Many popular Bible stories occurred during the week before Easter:

- **Jesus rode a donkey into Jerusalem as people shouted Hosanna!**
- **Jesus turned over the tables of money-changers in the temple.**
- **Jesus taught in the temple area.**
- **Jesus celebrated Passover with his disciples.**
- **Jesus was betrayed by Judas.**
- **Jesus prayed and was arrested in the Garden of Gethsemane.**
- **Jesus was brought before Pilate and King Herod.**
- **Jesus was crucified.**
- **Jesus was buried in the tomb.**
- **Jesus came back to life—the resurrection!**

 Activity

We are going to make an Easter Calendar and each day this week we will add an item to the calendar and talk about what was going on in Jesus' life on that day. Let's prepare the calendar and items for the coming week.

Create an eight-day calendar using a large piece of white construction paper or a piece of flip-chart paper. Divide the page into 8 sections or two rows of four sections each. Each section represents one day. Label the sections beginning with Palm Sunday and ending with Easter Sunday. Have the children color in the squares for each day with different colors.

Using the supplies listed under "Materials," make the following items for the calendar. Make items to fit the size of the squares on your calendar.

- **PALM LEAVES:** Cut out leaves from green construction paper.
- **TABLE AND MONEY:** Draw and cut out a "table" from brown construction paper. Glue two pennies on top of the table.
- **TEACHING SCROLLS:** Cut pipe cleaner into three two-inch sections. Roll and glue strips of paper onto the pipe cleaner sections so that a little pipe cleaner shows out each end.
- **PRAYING HANDS:** Trace a child's hand, fingers closed, on construction paper (brown or white). Cut out "praying hands" from construction paper.
- **COMMUNION:** Bread or cracker (cracker is easier to attach to the calendar).
- **CROSSES:** Make three crosses using glue and sticks.
- **TOMB:** Draw and cut out a tomb from black paper. Draw and cut a stone from brown paper.
- **LINENS:** Use small pieces of cloth to represent the burial linens.
- **ANGEL:** Use a picture of an angel or cut an angel from yellow paper.

Display the calendar by taping it on a wall or window in a prominent place. Starting with Palm Sunday, add a symbol to the calendar using glue and talk briefly about what the symbol represents. Read the section of scripture related to the event or tell the story using your own words.

Palm Sunday:	**Luke 19:28** "Palm leaves" to represent Jesus' triumphal entry into Jerusalem
Monday:	**Luke 19:45** "Table with money" Jesus drives out the money-changers.
Tuesday:	**Luke 19:47** "Scrolls" Jesus teaches at the temple.

Wednesday:	Empty Square: **We don't know everything Jesus did that week. What do you think Jesus would want to do during the last week of his life?**
Thursday:	**Luke 22:7** Communion and Judas' betrayal.
	Luke 22:39 Jesus prays in the Garden of Gethsemane.
Friday:	**Luke 23:26** Crucifixion. Three crosses.
Saturday:	**Luke 23:50** Tomb and stone. Jesus in the tomb.
Sunday:	**Luke 24:1** Resurrection. Linens and angel.

EXTRA EFFORT: Read about Easter week in the other gospels (Matthew, Mark, John) and add more detail to the calendar. For example, add the specific stories Jesus taught when he was in the temple. (Matthew 26-28; Mark 14-16; John 12-21.)

 Application

Easter is a special time when we remember that Jesus rose from the dead. In fact, it's such a special time that we have a celebration and make it a holiday. It's a privilege now to know that Jesus is in heaven preparing a place for us. Someday we too will go to heaven and spend time with him if we have asked Jesus to come into our hearts. God made that special plan for us.

Lesson 23:
A SHEPHERD KNOWS HIS SHEEP

 TEACHING GOAL: Jesus knows each of us by name.

1. Play theme song
2. Pray
3. Review last lesson
4. Lesson and discussion
5. Memorize: **When I played the blindfold game; I learned that Jesus knows my name.**
6. Close in prayer

 SCRIPTURE: John 10:3-14 "The watchman opens the gate for him, and the sheep listen to his voice. He calls his own sheep by name and leads them out. When he has brought out all his own, he goes on ahead of them, and his sheep follow him because they know his voice. But they will never follow a stranger; in fact, they will run away from him because they do not recognize a stranger's voice.... I am the good shepherd. The good shepherd lays down his life for the sheep.... I am the good shepherd; I know my sheep and my sheep know me."

 MATERIALS: Blindfold
Baby name book (You can check one out of a local library or even use the Internet.)

Words that are written in **bold** are when you, the parent, are speaking. Feel free to use your own words.

A Big Idea

In the Bible Jesus is compared to a shepherd and we are compared to sheep. Read the story from John 10. **Jesus says in the story that he is the shepherd and those who believe in him are his sheep. If Jesus is the shepherd, who is the stranger?** Satan.

There are people who do not believe that Jesus or God knows each one of us personally. But the Bible, God's Word, tells us that Jesus does know each of us by name.

 Activity

Blindfold one person at a time. Each family member takes a turn saying the name of the blindfolded person. The blindfolded person tries to guess who is saying his/her name. **How did you know who was saying your name?** I recognized your voices. **This represents Jesus who knows each of our names.**

Names have different meanings. Many names come from the Bible or have biblical meanings. Do you know what your name means? Using a baby name book, look up the names of family members and friends.

 Application

Why is it good to know that Jesus knows our names? Talk to kids about how knowing a name reveals a personal relationship. Tell kids about different impersonal ways people identify you without using your name. The fast food restaurant gives you a number. The government wants your social security number. The policeman wants your driver's license.

Maybe in our family we could just use numbers. I'll be number 3. You can be number 14. Have each child pick a number. Talk to each other and about each other for a few minutes and use numbers instead of names.

Reinforce the value of Jesus knowing us each by name.

Lesson 24:
THE MANGER

TEACHING GOAL: We can remember the birth of Jesus as we build a manger.

1. Play theme song
2. Pray
3. Review last lesson
4. Lesson and discussion
5. Memorize: **Jesus was born in a manger; God kept him from danger.**
6. Close in prayer

SCRIPTURE: Luke 2:7 "She wrapped him in cloths and placed him in a manger, because there was no room for them in the inn."

Matthew 1-2 and Luke 2

MATERIALS: 4 pieces of 2" x 2" x 24" wood
6 pieces of 1" x 4" x 18" wood
1 piece of 1" x 4" x 14" wood
Nails, Drill, Cardboard
Hay or straw
Doll and towel

Words that are written in **bold** are when you, the parent, are speaking. Feel free to use your own words.

A Big Idea

Tell the birth of Jesus story from Matthew 1-2 and Luke 2 using questions to help keep the children's attention. **What was the name of Jesus' mother?** Mary. **Father?** Joseph. God. **In what city was Jesus born?** Bethlehem. **Who came to visit Jesus?** Shepherds. Wise men. **When Jesus was born, where did he sleep?** A manger.

A manger is a feeding place for cattle. Talk about the different places we sleep and compare them to sleeping in a stable in a manger.

 Activity

BUILD A MANGER (Pre-drill the holes to make the nailing easier for children.) Cross two 2″ x 2″ x 24″ pieces of wood in an "X" and nail them in the center. Do the same with the other two pieces. These are your two major supports for the manger, one for each end. Next, using the six 1″ x 4″ x 18″ boards, create the trough by nailing them to the outside of the supports. It's best to do this on a curb or step so that you can lay the supports down on a flat surface to nail in the boards. Cut triangles of cardboard to fit at the ends and staple them firmly on the inside of the supports. Place the last board flat in the trough bottom to cover the gap at the bottom of the manger. Put hay in the manger. Wrap the doll in the towel and lay the towel in the manger.

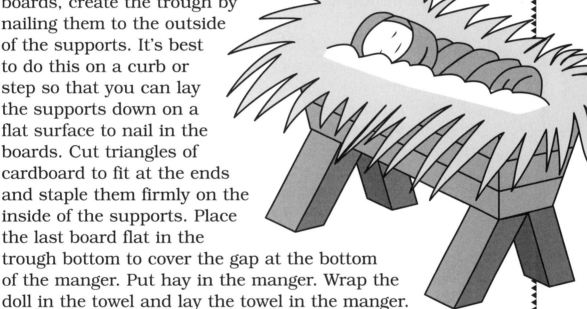

Application

We keep our manger next to the Christmas tree as a constant reminder that Christmas is a celebration of Jesus' birthday.

It's really a cow's eating dish. The next time you read or hear the Christmas story, remind the children of Jesus' humble beginning, that his first bed was a cow's eating dish.

Lesson 25:
EXCESS BAGGAGE

TEACHING GOAL: Satan wants to keep us from living a godly life.

1. Play theme song
2. Pray
3. Review last lesson
4. Lesson and discussion
5. Memorize: **Excess baggage gets in our way; from living a godly life today.**
6. Close in prayer

SCRIPTURE: Hebrews 12:1-2 "Therefore, since we are surrounded by such a great cloud of witnesses, let us throw off everything that hinders and the sin that so easily entangles, and let us run with perseverance the race marked out for us. Let us fix our eyes on Jesus, the author and perfecter of our faith."

Colossians 3:8 "But now you must rid yourselves of all such things as these: anger, rage, malice, slander, and filthy language from your lips."

1 Peter 2:1 "Therefore, rid yourselves of all malice and all deceit, hypocrisy, envy, and slander of every kind."

MATERIALS: Large coat
Adult-size pair of pants
Adult-size shoes

IN ADVANCE: This lesson is best done with another family or two. In advance tell others about your Family Time experience and invite them to join in with you for an evening. Not only will your friends enjoy having Family Time, but they may catch a vision for having their own regular Family Times too.

Words that are written in **bold** are when you, the parent, are speaking. Feel free to use your own words.

Big Idea

Make a list of "baggage," things that hinder us from living a godly life.

- Greed, taking something that is not yours

- Envy, jealousy

- Hatred

- Lying, covering up, being deceitful

- Anxiety, worry

- Bad language, gossip

- Unwillingness to forgive

 Activity

We call this the excess baggage race. After discussing the list you created, have a timed race. Have children run in regular clothes first. Then surprise them by bringing out the baggy clothes. One at a time, each child will put on the big clothes and race through an obstacle course (use chairs, boxes, etc. as the obstacles). Time them in both races, with normal clothes and excess baggage. Allow them to run an additional race in the baggy clothes for fun and then reinforce the principles of this lesson.

Did you run faster wearing the big clothes or your own?
My own. **What was it like to try to race while wearing the
baggy clothes?** It was hard, it slowed me down, tripped me.
**The baggy clothes represent "baggage," the list we just
made, things that keep us from doing what God has
asked of us.**

 Application

Read the scriptures listed on page 90 and ask the children
to listen for descriptions of things that hinder us.

Index

Seeing is Believing (ALL AGES)

Playing for Keeps (ALL AGES)

Running the Race (ALL AGES)

Wiggles, Giggles, & Popcorn (PRESCHOOLERS)

Index

Bubbles, Balloons, & Chocolate (PRESCHOOLERS)

Tried and True (TEENS)

www.famtime.com

Fun Spiritual Training in Your Home!

For All Ages

For Preschoolers

For Teens

Books in this series by Kirk Weaver

TOOLS FOR FAMILIES

- Free activities
- Activity books for children of all ages—
  Preschool, Elementary, Junior High, and
  High School

RESOURCES FOR CHURCHES

- Family Time Team Curriculum
- The Family Time Project: Equipping families
  through Sunday School, Vacation Bible
  School, mid-week programs

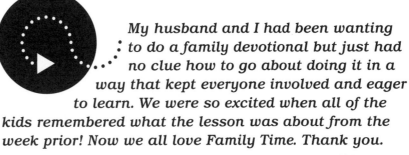

*My husband and I had been wanting
to do a family devotional but just had
no clue how to go about doing it in a
way that kept everyone involved and eager
to learn. We were so excited when all of the
kids remembered what the lesson was about from the
week prior! Now we all love Family Time. Thank you.*

—*K Lay*

Family Time Training
5511 S Youngfield St, Littleton, CO 80127
(303) 433-7010 • (866) 433-7010 (toll free)
info@famtime.com

You Will Benefit from
OTHER RESOURCES
for YOUR FAMILY

Discover practical, biblical tools to help you build strong bonds in your relationships at home. Find parenting books, CDs, and DVDs to help you parent from a heart-based perspective. Children's curriculum is available to teach your child the same concepts you are learning. **Free Email Parenting Tips** encourage you on a weekly basis. **Learn more at www.biblicalparenting.org.**

Free i
EMAIL PARENTING Tips

Receive practical, biblical parenting advice a couple times a week in your inbox. Sign up online at www.biblicalparenting.org. Also available in Spanish. Visit www.padresefectivos.org.

Sign up for Free Email Parenting Tips now.
(You can remove yourself from the list at any time.) Your email address will not be shared or sold to others.

NATIONAL CENTER for BIBLICAL PARENTING

To learn more give us a call or visit www.biblicalparenting.org.

76 Hopatcong Drive, Lawrenceville, NJ 08648-4136
Phone: (800) 771-8334
Email: parent@biblicalparenting.org